People of the Bible

The Bible through stories and pictures

Jonah
and the Great Fish

First published in the United States of America 1983
by Raintree Publishers, Inc.
205 West Highland Avenue, Milwaukee, Wisconsin 53203
in association with Belitha Press Ltd, London.

Conceived, designed and produced by Belitha Press Ltd,
40 Belitha Villas, London N1 1PD

Moody Press Edition 1984

ISBN 0-8024-0398-0

First published in Australia in paperback 1983
by Princeton Books Pty Ltd, PO Box 24, Cheltenham, Victoria 3192
in association with Raintree Childrens Books
205 West Highland Avenue, Milwaukee, Wisconsin 53203

ISBN 0-909091-21-8 (Australian)

Printed in Hong Kong by South China Printing Co.

Moody Press, a ministry of the Moody Bible Institute,
is designed for education, evangelization, and
edification. If we may assist you in knowing more
about Christ and the Christian life, please write us
without obligation: Moody Press, c/o MLM, Chicago,
Illinois 60610

Jonah and the Great Fish

Retold by Ella K. Lindvall
Pictures by Barry Wilkinson

MOODY PRESS
CHICAGO

There once was a man named Jonah, who
lived near the sea. One day he heard God tell
him, "Jonah, I want you to go to the great city
of Nineveh. Tell the people there that I see
what they are doing. They are so wicked that I
shall punish their city."

But Jonah thought, *Why should I help those people? Let them be punished. I won't go to Nineveh.*

Instead, Jonah went down to the harbor and found a ship to take him far away to a city called Tarshish. He bought his ticket and went on board the ship.

Aha! Jonah thought. *Soon the ship will sail. Then I shall get away from God and what He wants me to do.*

But Jonah was wrong. God knew what he was thinking and where he was.

After the ship was out on the sea, God sent a great storm. The wind blew hard. The waves rolled high.

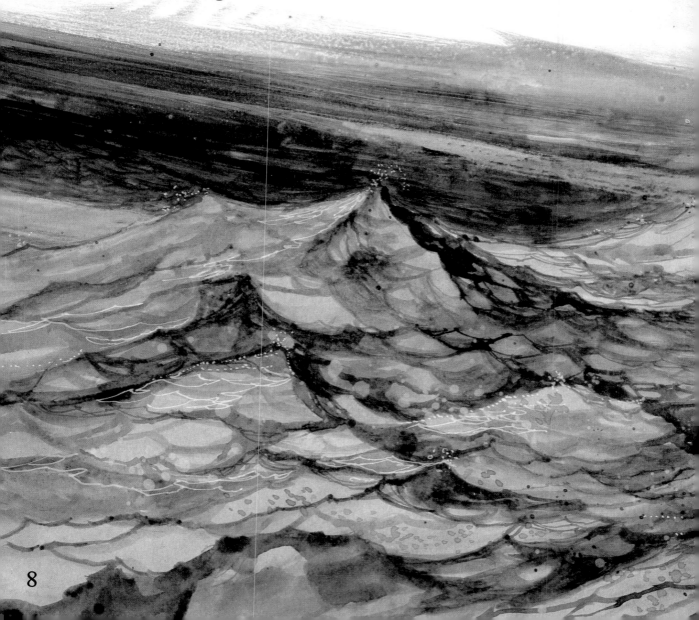

The sailors were terrified. *The ship will sink, and we shall drown,* they thought. So they threw some of the ship's load over the side to make the ship lighter.

Jonah did not know about the storm. He was down in the bottom of the ship, sleeping.

The captain himself woke him up. "What are you doing," he asked, "sleeping through this terrible storm? Get up and pray. Ask your God to stop the wind from blowing so hard, or else we are all going to die."

The sailors said, "God must be angry with someone who is on this ship. That is why such a bad storm has come. Let's draw lots to find out who it is."

Sure enough, when they looked at the lots in their hands, Jonah held the special one.

"Where do you come from?" the sailors asked him. "What is your work? Who are your people?"

"I am a Hebrew," said Jonah. "My God is the God of heaven, who made both the sea and the dry land."

Now the sailors were even more afraid. They knew Jonah was running away from God. He had told them.

"Just throw me into the sea," Jonah said. "I know this storm has come because of me."

The sailors did not want to throw Jonah into the sea. They rowed hard, trying to get the ship safely to shore.

15

But the storm only grew worse. At last the sailors saw that they would never be able to reach land. So they picked up Jonah and threw him into the great waves.

As Jonah fell down the side of the ship, the wind stopped. The waves became quiet. And the ship sailed safely on its way.

Down, down, down went Jonah into the deep sea. But Jonah did not drown. He found himself going into the mouth of a huge fish. The fish gulped, and Jonah went straight down into its belly.

Did God send that fish? Yes, He did.

Jonah was very frightened. He prayed to God from inside the fish.

"Please, God, help me! You have sent me down to the bottom of the sea. The huge waves rolled over me. Seaweed wrapped itself around my head. I nearly died. Lord, hear my voice!"

Could God hear a man praying from deep in the sea? Yes, He could.

And God listened to Jonah. He said to the great fish, "Spit up Jonah now and see that he comes out of your mouth onto the dry land."

The fish heard what God said, and he spit up
Jonah onto a beach.

"Get up now and go to Nineveh," the Lord
said to Jonah. "Tell that great city the words I
will give you."

This time Jonah did what he was told.

When he came to Nineveh, Jonah said, "I have come to warn you. Forty days from now God will punish your city because you are so wicked."

The king of Nineveh heard Jonah's warnings, and he was afraid. He took off his fine clothes and put on a robe of sackcloth to show that he was sorry.

He told his people, "You must wear sackcloth like me. We all must turn from our wicked ways. We must tell God we are sorry."

Then the king said, "Let none of us eat—not even the animals. Put sackcloth on them too. And let everyone start doing what is right."

When God saw that the people of Nineveh were sorry, He did not punish them.

For God loved the people of Nineveh even though they were wicked, and He knew when they were truly sorry.

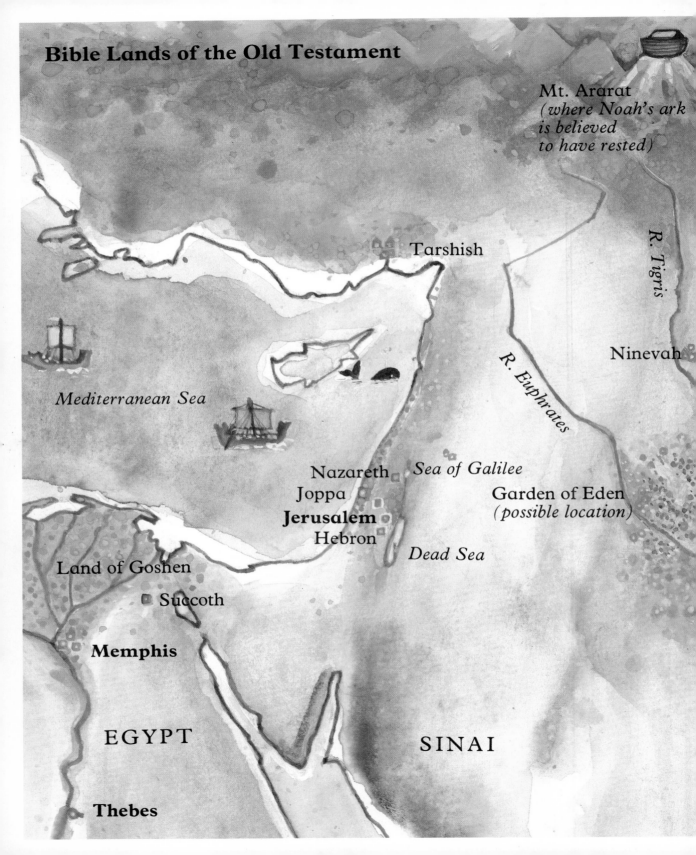

Bible Lands of the Old Testament

Mt. Ararat
*(where Noah's ark
is believed
to have rested)*

Tarshish

R. Tigris

Ninevah

R. Euphrates

Mediterranean Sea

Nazareth   *Sea of Galilee*

Joppa   Garden of Eden
                        (possible location)
Jerusalem

Hebron

Dead Sea

Land of Goshen

Succoth

Memphis

EGYPT   SINAI

Thebes